Hip-Hop Dance

By Trudy Becker

level
2
little blue
readers

www.littlebluehousebooks.com

Little Blue House is distributed by North Star Editions:
sales@northstareditions.com | 888-417-0195

Produced for Little Blue House by Red Line Editorial.

Photographs ©: iStockphoto, cover, 4, 7, 9, 13, 16, 19, 21, 24 (top left), 24 (top right), 24 (bottom right); Shutterstock Images, 10, 14–15, 23, 24 (bottom left)

Library of Congress Control Number: 2022919919

ISBN
978-1-64619-830-6 (hardcover)
978-1-64619-859-7 (paperback)
978-1-64619-914-3 (ebook pdf)
978-1-64619-888-7 (hosted ebook)

Printed in the United States of America
Mankato, MN
082023

About the Author

Trudy Becker lives in Minneapolis, Minnesota. She likes exploring new places and loves anything involving books.

Table of Contents

Spin and Turn

One kid dances in the middle of a crowd.

He spins and turns.

He balances on his hands and makes a shape in the air.

A girl listens to the music and dances.
All of her moves have high energy.
She moves her feet quickly.

A group dances together.
The kids do the same
moves but use their
own style.
They are dancing
hip-hop.

All About It

Hip-hop dance is part of a group of art forms called hip-hop.

It is part of Black culture and started in New York City.

Break dancing is part of
hip-hop dance.
Dancers make shapes
with their bodies.
They need good balance
and fast feet.

Hip-hop dance uses simple moves too. People can repeat them. They can use these moves when listening to hip-hop music.

Learning How

Some people learn hip-hop dance with their friends. Some take lessons. They perform on stages or streets.

Hip-hop dancers practice their moves.
The moves should look amazing and show their feelings.

Hip-hop dancers can wear different things. Many wear loose clothes. They might wear hats. The clothing and dances both show their style.

Before performing,

dancers get ready.

They loosen up.

They check the music.

It is time for

hip-hop dance!

Glossary

balance

hat

crowd

lesson

Index